Photography:

Digital SLR Crash Course!

Master Digital Photography & Take Amazing Photographs for Beginners

Contents

Demystifying Photography

From A distance, photography appears like a complex career. Yet, if you took a closer look, it really is the same old wine in new wineskins. It is actually possible to practice photography from a self-taught angle. It is not as confusing as it seems. Modern digital cameras can appear intimidating thanks to the many features that many of us don't even know how to use; let's be honest, most of us know how to press the shutter button and how to zoom!

In order to understand digital photography better, it is important that you know that digital photography basically resolves around how the three elements of the exposure triangle i.e. shutter speed, ISO and aperture relate to each other.

To begin with, let us start with familiarizing ourselves with these and more terms and aspects of photography that really form the basis of photography. These concepts determine whether you will be a success story as a photographer or a quack who always complains about how his or her camera is not working as advertised in the ad.

Shutter Speed

The shutter can be described as a flap that opens and closes when you shoot photos. It is right at the front side of your camera. The aperture is a small opening that allows light to hit the lens of the camera and the shutter speed is the time it takes between the opening and closing of the shutter. Shutter speed is measured in fractions of a second. The faster the shutter speed, the clearer the images you capture in motion. Fast shutter speeds freeze motion making them perfect for action photography especially if you don't want the photos to look blurry.

Nonetheless, both slow and fast shutter speeds have their uses in photography. Slow shutter speeds leave a blur, especially when capturing photos in motion. High shutter speed is ideal for capturing images of wildlife in motion. In particular, you would have great images of wildcats in speedy chases. You would also be able to capture great images of birds in flight when you use fast shutter speeds.

Fortunately, modern digital cameras can adjust shutter speeds to suit your purpose. Slow shutter speeds are ideal for capturing scenery and fixed objects. If you adjust the shutter speed, you can create special effects on the photos. For instance, when capturing natural scenery that includes a water fall, adjusting the shutter to be slower allows for the illusion of motion to manifest. So, how do you set the shutter speed so that you can derive the most benefits?

Setting the Shutter Speed

There is a strong correlation between the shutter speed and the aperture size. When you set your camera to shutter priority, it allows you to manually adjust the shutter speed while your camera determines the aperture.

If on the other hand you set the camera to manual mode, you are allowed to set both the shutter speed and the aperture. You can play around with the settings when capturing photos in different situations so that you master how to use the camera appropriately at different times.

ISO

ISO refers to the cameras level of sensitivity to light. A low ISO means that your camera is less sensitive to light and vice versa. The image sensor is an item of great importance in photography. A high ISO corrupts your images with a lot of grain added. Low ISO captures photos without grain; you can choose either based on what you want to achieve in photography.

On your camera calibration, the ISO setting increases in a geometric progression based on a factor of 2. The lowest ISO is 100. It increases to 200x, 400x, 800x etc where 800x, represents high sensitivity in this illustration and 100, low sensitivity.

High ISO setting is good for capturing images in motion. On the other hand, you can use the base ISO to capture quality images in an environment with sufficient lighting.

Aperture on Camera Lens

Aperture refers simply to the opening of the lens through which light passes. It is calibrated in f/stops and is generally written as numbers such as 1.4, 2, 2.8, 4, 5.6, 8, 11 and 16.

The lower the f/stop—the larger the opening in the lens—the less depth of field—the blurrier the background.

The higher the f/stop—the smaller the opening in the lens—the greater the depth of field—the sharper the background.

This may seem a little contradictory at first but will become clearer as you take pictures at varying f/stops.

DSLR

The initials stand for Digital Singular Lens Reflex. This camera uses mirrors to reflect light to the viewfinder. The viewfinder is the hole you look through to see the image of the object you wish to capture.

In a nutshell, a DSLR constitutes of:

#Lens

#Matte focusing screen,

#Condensers

#Shutter

#Reflex mirror

#Image sensor

#Pentaprism

#Viewfinder

How the DSLR works

You view your image through the viewfinder; this is a hole at the back of the camera where you see the image that you want to capture. Light is reflected onto the reflex mirror via a lens. The pentaprism in turn transforms the vertical light to horizontal light and directs it to the viewfinder. The pentaprism is located inside your camera right behind the shutter and lens.

Once you take your picture by pressing the shutter button, the reflex mirror moves up and allows light to pass. The action simultaneously blocks the vertical channel then the shutter opens and then light strikes the sensor. The shutter closes and causes the reflex mirror to move back.

Now that you have some basic understanding of how DSLRs work, you probably would want to know how to compose nice photos while taking advantage of the exposure triangle to the fullest.

How to Compose Excellent Photos - Top Composition Rules

The Rule of Thirds

Observing the rule of thirds ensures that your photograph generates interest to the viewer. Imagine that your target image is split into nine equal parts with two vertical and two horizontal lines. It has been established that placing your image right at the intersections of these imaginary lines creates more interest as opposed to centering. It creates a balance in your images. In fact, the rule is so widely used in modern day photography that some camera manufacturers have included features that enable you to capture images that way without trying to apply it off head. Such cameras provide the option of superimposing the grid lines on the image before you take your shot. If you are using such a camera, carefully place the image at the intersections of these vertical and horizontal lines and compare with others you don't.

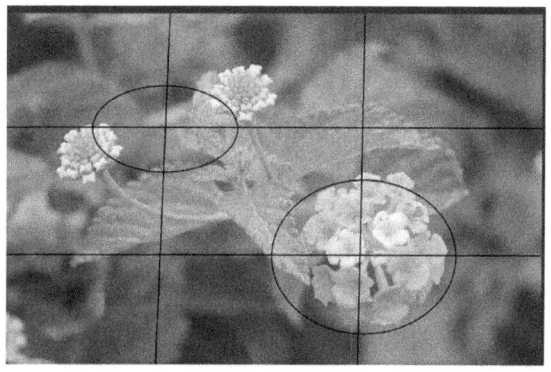

Avoid the Centre

There is a tendency for photography beginners to want to place all their images right at the center of the frame. If you took time to study some of the most striking photos in newspapers, magazines and even online, you will discover that professional photographers try to avoid the center as much they can. Placing an image at the center may suggest that it is your most important target but it is a boring way of doing it. Although drifting away from the center, such as applying the rule of thirds seems to leave a vacuum at the center, you can fill up such empty space by inserting an object of less importance in the photo. This technique is effective in utilizing the rule of thirds and solving the central emptiness concern.

Move Closer To your Image

Moving closer to the target object of interest, helps you capture clear photos. In addition, it makes it much easier to eliminate what you do not need in the photo.

Simplify the Scene

The basic inspiration behind taking any shot is the subject of interest. Therefore, it is critical to identify your subject so that you only include images that support the story of the subject. Choose settings that target the subject and can discriminate other objects. Once you have successfully chosen your target, and selected a suitable zoom level (depending on your lens), try to place the rest of the objects in the background of the shot or push them out of focus. If you do not wish to keep other objects in the background or omit them, then make them part of the story you are telling with your subject image.

It is important to learn that simplifying your scene makes your photos have a clear theme. It is actually an effective way to eliminate clutter in photography. You do not want to take photos, which leave the viewer wondering what exactly they are supposed to see. Your photograph should speak for itself. In any case, you will not be there to always explain what your intention was. You need to live up to the reputation of a photo. It is said that a picture is worth a thousand words so save the print space with nicely taken photographs with clear themes.

Fill the Frame

A frame is what encloses your point of focus in a photo. Filling the frame of your shot strikes a balance of utility. By filling the frame, you make the subject of your photo look larger while ensuring that you cut down on clutter/distracters in the photo. Voids act as detractors in photography. The problem of empty space in a frame can be quite a challenge if you tried to do it on your own. One of the most common features of empty space is empty skies. Naturally, empty skies reduce the object size; making it less significant to the viewer. This is a rather tricky scenario to handle because you may not have an option to deal with it at the time of taking the shot. Although you can use post processing software to adjust and optimize your photos, you can reduce this distraction or eliminate it by zooming in or moving closer to the target object. You can zoom in to help focus your perspective of the shot at hand. Moving closer exposes more detail and makes your image more interesting to view. This solution will only apply if you have both the opportunity and the liberty to move freely around your target subject otherwise the post processing option is your image salvager.

Use Leading Lines

The concept of lines can be quite confusing to a beginning photographer, yet it is simple enough to master within a few practice shots. The lines in photography are not actual lines as we know them in ordinary language but in photography, objects that take linear shapes in the background are referred to as lines. There are many lines we can utilize in photography. Examples include buildings, electricity lines, roads, walls, fences etc. The linear shapes vary and, of course deliver varying effects. They may be wavy, curved or straight lines. It also depends on your intention to take the photo. For instance, vertical lines often communicate a sense of performance, peace, power, height, strength, solidarity, dominance, integrity substance etc. while horizontal lines speak out a sense of relaxation, calm, width, stability, security, and constancy.

It has been established that lines help to guide the viewer in a certain direction. As you view the target image through the viewfinder of your camera, try to place the image relative to these lines so that your images do not appear out of tune with their natural surrounding.

The central role of using these lines is to converge the focus of the viewer. Note that you can also create an imaginary line that successfully guides a focus. For example, using an off center image that is facing a particular direction can lead the image viewer to the intended target.

When you want to use leading lines, you should ensure that you use narrow aperture in order to create a large depth of field so that you can bring everything that needs to be in the photo into good focus. When you use leading lines, you are ideally shifting the focus of the viewer from foreground items to the background items in the photo. As such, you have to make sure that the items in the foreground are in clear focus. With leading lines, you can:

*Lead a viewer from one photo object in the photo to the next

*Keep the focus of the viewer on one part of the photo

Use Diagonals

Incidentally, the lines serve more purposes than simply directing the viewer to a subject of interest in a shot. Lines create effects too. You can use these to tell your story. Horizontal lines create a calm and static effect. You can use these to create a very strong sense of movement or depth. Vertical lines create a feeling of stability and permanence, while diagonals are your best bet at creating a sense of drama and action. They evoke a sense of motion and uncertainty. All these effects add tremendous value to your images. Although you cannot necessarily have them in one photo, you have the prerogative to choose one that will capture your message and send it to the viewer without strain.

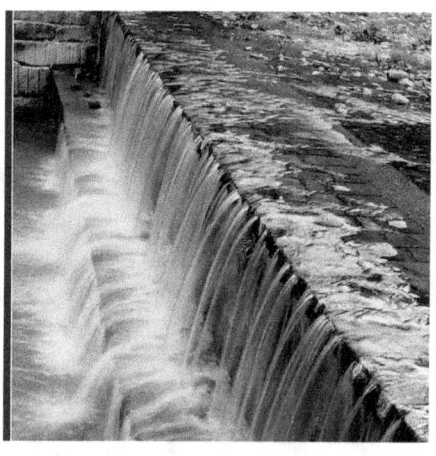

You can successfully achieve the diagonal lines by tilting your camera slightly to change horizontal and vertical lines into horizontal lines in order to bring out the needed effect. You can also use the zig zag effect if you are using diagonals in your patterns. When you repeat the pattern, you help drag the eye into the image over a larger area within the frame.

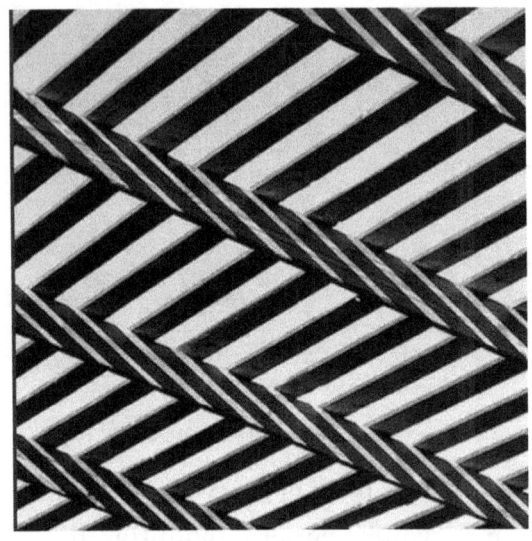

You can get wider angle views by making use of the wide angle lenses. With these lenses, you have the freedom to tilt and shift to enjoy more from the target scene.

The Dutch Tilt Technique

In this technique, you get your unique angles by slowly tilting your camera as you take the photo. The resultant images are often unique and capture special feelings.

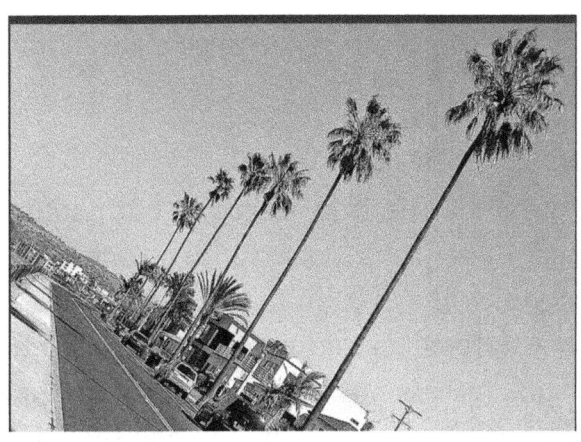

Create Space to Move

A good photo portrays a sense of motion. Create a sense of motion in your photos by ensuring that your subject has space to move, usually ahead of them. You can achieve this by first ensuring that your subject is not close to the frame.

If you take time to observe the common photos we see every day such as those on bill boards, the clever creation of space for the subjects helps us follow the movement/ glance of the subject. Your subject needs space to look somewhere or move somewhere, as this adds life in the image and eliminates the sense of a dead scene. It is advisable to create more space ahead of the photo than behind it.

Backgrounds

Backgrounds can make or break your photo. You should therefore be alert and proactive about what you will accept in the background of your shot. Cluttered backgrounds spoil your image. You can successfully discriminate what appears in the background by manipulating the angle of view and shifting position. Using a wide lens aperture is a helpful aid in selecting the objects to include in the background.

Alternatively, make use of the zoom feature to push the undesirable objects out of focus. Again, the selection of a background should be influenced by the story you want to tell. Decide whether a background should be part of your story or not.

Colors

Although primary colors are effective in attracting attention, they have been used for long and in far too many themes. You can take a different approach by splashing color on the background that is monochromatic. The secret behind effective color manipulation lies in your ability to isolate and frame subjects uniquely.

Break the Rules Sometimes

If you know the rules, you may have to spontaneously break them. However, it is critical that you first know which rule you should break in a given scene. Although rules have shaped photography over the years and have provided a basis to assert photography as an independent discipline with its foundations on a body of knowledge, the beauty of photography also comes from deviating from the norm and embracing spontaneity.

It is not uncommon to see amazing photographs that have not observed any of the rules. Yet, it is critical to first master the rules so that you break them for a purpose. Usually, the spontaneous photos that draw attention seek to convey specific messages. Therefore, instead of going on a wild guess trip with your photography, learn the rules first, and then break them deliberately because you want to convey a message.

The bottom-line is that photography is an art. As with all other types of art, creativity and spontaneity are never far from the practice.

Trying to cage photography with strict rules is simply untenable. You soon witness instances, which blatantly defy the rules and still make great shots all the same.

So, now that you understand some important image composition rules that you should observe or even break when you want to, let's now delve into details on how to embrace the full power of framing to get the best photos that tell exactly what you want to say.

Master how to use wide appeal

If you are doing portrait photography, you should ideally be focusing more on the eyes. By placing them at the center of your frame, you will probably end up with a lot of space just above the head of your subject. As such, you should aim towards keeping the eyes along the top horizontal line. If your subject is strategically placed on one side, ensure that they don't look straight into the edge of your image. So if they are looking towards the right side of the frame, ensure that they stand along the vertical line in order to ensure that they only look into the space that is at the right of the frame.

Don't shy away from using this similar technique to capture action photos.

Mastering the Art of Framing Photos

The basic reason for using frames is to focus attention on the important parts of a photograph while blocking out parts of the photo that you don't want to put too much emphasis on. Through framing, you can:

*Intrigue the viewer

*Drive the viewer towards specific objects of focus i.e. the main focal point

*Give context to images

Framing can be achieved through shooting across doorways, tunnels, overhanging branches, windows, arches and many other places that help give more emphasis on what you want to focus on.

In modern digital photography, you can use wide-angle lenses to frame photos thanks to their versatility and ability to manipulate photograph scenes. With, the wide-angle, you can get a wide view that ensures that you capture everything you want in a given scene. Moreover, they provide you with advanced features that make it easy to select what you want to remain within the frame. Additionally, you can use these lenses to make close objects look closer in the image and the distant objects look much smaller than they actually are. With that, you can create a perfect distance and scale illusion that helps bring out the intended effect of focusing your attention on one object within the photo as opposed to other objects that may not be the center of attention.

Another advantage with using wide-angle lenses is that they enable you to capture wider depths in a shot field. You keep the details you want within focus. You can have what you want without making too many decisions as to distance and angle for the best and clear shot. Here are some helpful tips you should observe when framing photos.

#Foreground: When you are carrying out landscape photography, provide elements that draw interest in the foreground with the wide-angle lenses. They help you fill the vacuum created by distant images.

#Aspect Ratio: Choose either portrait or landscape, depending on the surrounding. If it's a wide image, go for landscape. Portrait is ideal for close-ups and pictures of people. The idea behind choosing the correct aspect ratio is to eliminate background noise (noise is the element you inadvertently include in your shot).

#Using Lines: You can skillfully guide the viewer of your photo to a subject or around the photo by careful use of lines. Use your wide-angle lens to identify the lines in the field of view.

Image Manipulation Tips and Tricks

If you wish to excel in any trade, there are 3 basic things you must grasp; knowledge, skill and experience. However, the element that really sets you apart from the rest of the pack is aspect of tricks of the trade. Here are some tips and tricks that will lift your photography a notch higher.

From whose point of view are you shooting?

Point of view simply means the position from where you are capturing the photos; the subject could be above you, below you, or close to you. You need to realize that the point of view from which you capture the photos will determine how anybody is going to see the photos. When you are shooting an insect, you should capture a photo while you are looking up as opposed to looking down on it. If you are shooting a bird on trees, you should shoot an eye level bird shot.

You can also create a great point of view by thinking of yourself as the subject such that you capture photos from the subject's angle. For instance, if you are shooting a chef preparing a meal, you want to capture the image from the chef's point of view. In this case, you will be capturing the photos from the eyes of the chef. This is one of the best tips and tricks for creating a connection between the viewer and the subject.

Also, when shooting short people, it is best to shoot from below if you don't want to focus too much on how short they really are. When you shoot from below, it creates a sense of dominance such that the viewer feels inferior to the subject. The opposite is also true.

Know how to use exposure compensation

Unless you are shooting on manual mode, the camera will automatically set itself to specify the exposure of the photo to light depending on how lit or dark the surrounding environment is. The exposure compensation button is usually marked +/-. When you press '+', you make an image brighter but when you press '-', you make the image appear darker.

You can adjust the exposure compensation in 1/3 and ½ EV or stops with each stop adjustment doubling or halving the amount of light that gets to the image sensor depending on whether the EV is fixed at -1 or +1. When you set an exposure compensation adjustment of +1 EV, you will have an image that is twice as bright as base exposure while an exposure compensation fixed at -1 EV makes the image half as bright as the base exposure.

You can fix exposure compensation with ease whether you are shooting on shutter speed priority mode, aperture priority mode or program mode (these three are the "auto modes for the pros"). When shooting on Program mode (P on the camera), your camera will adjust the shutter speed or the aperture so that it can accommodate adjustments on the exposure compensation.

For instance, dropping the shutter speed to 1/125s will make your camera to double the amount of light that passes through the sensor since the exposure takes twice as long. Additionally, when you open the aperture to f/4, your camera will double the amount of light that reaches the sensor given that the aperture will be opened at full stop. It is the work of the camera's processor to determine the values it should adjust in program mode (in doing so, it could consider such things like focal length of the lens and max lens aperture.

When shooting on aperture priority mode, the aperture will remain constant at whatever setting you have fixed but adjust the shutter speed in order to accommodate the adjustments in exposure compensation. On the other hand, if you are shooting on shutter speed priority mode, the camera's shutter speed remains fixed while the aperture adjusts when exposure compensation is adjusted.

Note: When shooting on either shutter speed priority or aperture priority, your camera should adjust the ISO especially if you have fixed the ISO to automatic mode.

White balance mastery

Although most cameras will adjust automatically to correct white balance depending on the surroundings, you can figure out how to manipulate your photos for a better quality image that speaks everything about the shooting. For instance, such things like the kind of color in the surroundings determine how your photo will be. As such, you should understand how you are going to work with the light to your benefit. Tungsten produces yellow, fluorescent produces a slightly green color while sunlight gives out blue. You should adjust the white balance especially if you are shooting in an environment that has mixed lightings. Your DSLR camera will probably have a WB button, which you can use to adjust the lighting of your camera based on the prevailing light. For instance, use tungsten when shooting in an area with the normal bulb that produces a sort of yellow light, fluorescent in an area light with fluorescent, sunlight in sunny environments etc. Other settings include cloudy, flash, shade etc.

Trick: Try shooting your photos at different settings of white balance until you find what works for you.

Use flash to your advantage

Don't just have flash enabled all the times because it could ruin your photos. Actually, before you can use flash, you should take a few steps back then zoom in to achieve an excellent framing. You can then check the flash compensation feature or the flash power so that you can achieve greater white balance.

The mode works magic

When you are shooting fast action, you should set your camera to work on shutter priority then increase the shutter speed so that you can freeze motion when taking photos. As such, you will be sure that you won't capture blurry photos or miss important moments because the shutter speed was not fast enough. However, if you are shooting in lower light, you should set your camera to aperture priority since this will ensure that enough light passes through the sensor. In other instances, you can opt to close the iris of the lens especially if you are capturing landscapes while using a tripod to help enhance the depth of field.

Get a flash diffuser

If you cannot dial down the power of the flash, you can instead opt to get a diffuser to help spread the light. A simple piece of wax paper placed on the flash can be all you need to get started. If you are using a DSLR, an empty film canister will do.

Let light work for you

Don't shoot photos while the sun is right at the back of the subject if you are taking outdoor photos. Likewise, use flash when shooting photos in front of a monument or a landmark where you cannot move. The flash will fill in the shadows.

Watch out for what you keep in the background

The background of your image adds to the narrative of the subject. Crop and exclude any elements that may cause distraction to the viewer. You can do this by use of the various shooting techniques, including the fish eye and close up shots.

Avoid bland skies

These can be a terrible distraction and boring addition to your picture.

#Check ISO setting especially when lighting conditions change and at the beginning of the photo shoot. Adjust these when beginning any shooting session.

#Try full manual setting sometimes. You never learn until you err. Make a habit of deliberately leaving your camera on manual mode so that you can try to remember the settings for particular scenes.

#Use the custom setting for the best color results on your images.

Another useful tip you need to bear in mind all the time in your manipulation process is the need to pay special attention to heights, shadows, and reflections before you merge the layers. Note that any matter affects the direction of light in an image. Mirrors alter the direction of light while solid bodies determine the position and direction of shadows.

How to Make the Best Use of the Lens and Filters

One key feature of DSLRs is the fact that they have interchangeable lenses, which means that you can try using different lenses for shooting different objects. Experimentation will definitely help greatly. However, before you can start feeling overwhelmed by the endless possibilities of how you can shoot photos, here are a few tips to help you get started.

Use the lens to create an illusion of depth of field

You should add a little creativity to your background and immediate foreground to help create an illusion of depth of field.

Take advantage of the sun flare

Instead of trying to blur the background with little or no success, you can try to shoot when the sun is right at the back of the subject in order to blur the background. However, don't just shoot at the sun otherwise your photo will be too blurred.

Try using texture for the background

Try to capture a nice texture so that you can enhance it without requiring too much depth of field. You can as well add a storyline to the background. Try to be artistic with your shots; don't just focus too much on the subject until you miss out on the surroundings. You can tell a story with the image using the background items.

Get closer to the subject

Don't be too shy to get close to the subject; ensure that you get close enough to fill the frame with the subject. Whichever lens you are using, getting closer doesn't hurt; you don't necessarily have to always use the zoom all the time.

Make use of filters

Filters have been likened to sunglasses. You wear them to limit the amount of light that enters your eye. Similarly, sunglasses not only protect your eye against harsh bright light but also protect your eye. In addition, they provide an aesthetic value in some circumstances. The lens is a delicate accessory on your digital camera. It requires as much protection from damage by the elements as your eye needs;

hence, the need for a filter. Filters also protect your lenses against scratches and dust. Like your sunglasses, the lens filters influence the colors the viewer can see in an image. In general, filters provide you with a better view of images in intense light. The ability to reduce reflections is handy in enhancing the quality of your images. Filters have a wide range of uses even beyond the list below:

*Reduce reflections in an image

*Protect lenses

*Improve the quality of your photo in poor lighting

*Enhance colors

Filters are necessary for modifying light that enters the lens. Although some photographers think that the existence of Photoshop and light room is a perfect replacement for filters, it is evident that there are some effects that cannot be edited or manipulated in post processing with such softwares. In fact, some filters help to improve post-processing results.

It is however necessary to reiterate at this point that just like how you use your sunglasses, you must carefully select the filters depending on the prevailing conditions for taking shots. Generally, the existing filters can be grouped into the following categories.

*UV/clear/haze: protects against moisture, dust and scratch

*Polarizing filters: these serve to protect the lens against polarizing light

*Neutral density filters

-Hard edge graduated neutral density filter

-Soft edge graduated neutral density filters

-Reverse graduated neutral density filters

*Color/warming/cooling filters

*Close up filters; also referred to as dioptors

*Special effects filters

You should select a filter that will serve you best based on the prevailing circumstances.

How to Avoid Ruining Your Photos

Many photographers become frustrated because they fall into the trap of committing very common mistakes in photography. Many of these mistakes are more of discipline and behavior mistakes than real photography problems. In fact, many of them can be corrected by applying common sense and a little insight; something you certainly can do if you have a burning intent to succeed in photography. A few others are technical ignorance and omissions.

Let us have the list of the mistakes at a glance before we explain the details

*Tendency to always shoot at eye level

*Not getting close enough

*Small aperture adjustment

*Ignorance of camera controls and missing the shot

*Shooting without a tripod in low light or at night

*Unpreparedness then missing the opportunity and the shot

*Ignorance of light effects; shooting at the wrong time of day

*Using the camera flash

We will discuss some of these mistakes in greater detail just to help you understand

Not Getting Close Enough

Getting close to the image unveils more interesting features about your subject. Do not fumble and guess about what the best distance is. Just focus, look into your camera and make a decision based on the image you see in the frame.

However, the best way to master the distance you need for your best shot is by practicing. You do not have to worry about the cost of replacing exposures anymore. You can take as many shots as you wish for practice and delete them as you need to. Nothing beats practice. Take test shots and analyze results.

Small Aperture Adjustment

Do not set the aperture too small- it leads to a slow shutter speed. The aperture and shutter speed require a balance. When you select a high f/number such as f/11, the shutter speed slows to unacceptable range for hand held shooting.

*You should keep the shutter speed faster than 1 divided by the focal length of the lens.

This way, you avoid making your images look blurry.

Tendency to Shoot From Eye Level Vintage

Eye level pictures are fine, but they render no news. You stand a better chance of success if you realize and embrace the need to get creative and experiment with new perspectives and angles. Try out such perspectives as the bird's eye view, close ups and worm's view. You will realize that your image reflects different subtle qualities with each changing perspective.

Ignorance of Camera Buttons

Try to master the buttons of your camera by observing them and reading the manual carefully. Practice is all you need to master the location and functions of each button on your camera.

Unpreparedness

Do not pay too much attention in caring for the camera and miss the shot. Do not keep your camera in its case when you expect to take shots. Leave the camera lens open. It is a common phenomenon to see some photographers fumbling with their cameras because the lens cap is closed but they are not aware.

Not using tripod in low light

Just don't make excuses. Use your tripod to take better photos in poor lighting conditions.

Shooting At the Wrong Time

If your shot can wait, wait for the opportune time. Do not shoot at midday when there is harsh light. It will not only ruin your images but has the potential to damage your camera lens. Try shooting at dusk or in the morning when the rays are relatively soft.

Using the Camera Flash

Mistake 1: Not using flash

One of the biggest mistakes that photographers make is to not use their flash.

In many cases this is because they don't understand how to use it or are unaware of the benefits that flash photography can bring.

Flash is not something that should only be used when there's not enough light to shoot without it, it's also extremely useful in bright lighting conditions because it can fill-in deep shadows and help you balance the exposure of your subject with that of the background

Mistake 2: Using flash with distant subjects

At the other end of the scale from not using flash, this is a common problem for photographers who use their camera on the automatic settings or who wildly overestimate the power of the flash.

You see it a lot a stadium events where the crowd seems to sparkle with all the flashes going off.

Even the light from a powerful flashgun will not illuminate a subject at the centre of a stadium if you're shooting from the crowd.

Mistake 3: Red eye

Redeye in portraits is caused by light entering the subject's eye and bouncing back from the retina into the lens.

Most cameras offer a redeye reduction mode that works by firing a pre-flash that causes the pupil to close down before the main flash and the exposure.

This can work well, but it doesn't always cure the problem completely.

Another solution is to position the flash further away from the lens so that the light doesn't bounce straight back down the barrel.

Naturally, this can't be done with the on-camera flash and instead an external flashgun, which is connected to the camera either wirelessly or by a cord, is used.

In some cases, simply using a hot-shoe mounted flashgun rather than a camera's pop-up flash can be enough because the light source is raised sufficiently above the lens.

Mistake 4: Killing the atmosphere

While a burst of flash can illuminate dark shadows, it can also destroy the atmosphere of a low-light scene.

In some cases it may be better to turn off the flash and extend the shutter speed and if necessary put the camera on a tripod, or push up the sensitivity setting to produce a more natural looking image.

Alternatively, check your flashgun (or camera's manual) and find out how to adjust the flash exposure compensation so that you can reduce the amount of light that it pushes out.

You could also combine this with a longer exposure (using the slow sync flash mode) so that the background records a little while your nearby subject is illuminated by a small burst of flash.

Bonus Content!

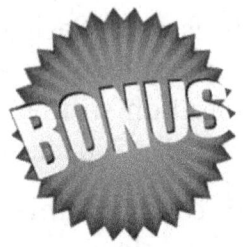

As a token of our appreciation Grand Reveur Publications would like to give you access to our exclusive bonus content (including free eBooks!).
You're only a click away from receiving:

Exclusive pre-release access to our latest eBooks
Free Grand Reveur eBooks during promotional periods
A method ANYONE can use to publish their own book and make passive income

https://ignorelimits.leadpages.net/grandreveur publications/

As this is a limited time offer it would be a shame to miss out, I recommend grabbing these bonuses before reading on.